A **Golden Books** OUTDOOR ACTION GUIDE

W9-CKW-127
WITHDRAWN

CAMPING

**by
CORINNE
HUMPHREY
&
CHEYENNE ROUSE**

Golden Books
New York

Mount Laurel Library
100 Walt Whitman Avenue
Mt. Laurel, N.J. 08054-9539
(609) 234-7319

© **1997 Golden Books Publishing Company, Inc.**
No part of this book may be reproduced or copied in any
form without written permission from the copyright owner.
Printed in U.S.A.

DRYLOFT® and GORE-TEX® are
registered trademarks of W. L.
Gore & Associates, Inc.
COLEMAN® is a registered
trademark of The Coleman
Company, Inc. POLARTEC® is a
registered trademark of ADS
Properties Corp. ACE® is a
registered trademark of Becton,
Dickinson and Company.
BENADRYL® is a registered
trademark of Warner-Lambert
Company. HUNGRY JACK® is a
registered trademark of The
Pillsbury Company. M&M's® is
a registered trademark of
Mars, Incorporated. LAWRY'S®
is a registered trademark of
Lawry's Investments, Inc.

All other trademarks are the property of
Golden Books Publishing Company, Inc.
850 Third Avenue
New York, NY 10022

Art Director: Kate Kriege
Design: McDill Design
Editor: Tricia Friel
Thanks to the following people and
companies for their help:

Jodi Mantel,
Cedarburg, Wisconsin

Johnson Worldwide
Associates,
Racine, Wisconsin

ISBN: 0-307-24601-9

ABOUT THE AUTHORS

Corinne Humphrey was raised in the Blue Ridge Mountains of Virginia, and the love of the outdoors was instilled early by her parents with frequent camping trips locally and at many of the National Parks across the U.S. In addition to the wealth of experience from those early years, she has planned and conducted bicycle camping trips in New England, walking tours in Europe, and camping excursions around the West.

Corinne is a published photographer and travel writer who roams the world gathering material for her articles. Her work has appeared in such magazines as *Four Seasons Travel, Persimmon Hill, France,* and others. She is currently at work on an outdoor cookbook. Corinne makes her home in Cardiff-by-the-Sea, California.

Cheyenne Rouse, co-author, is also a professional photographer who specializes in adventure sports, outdoor lifestyles, and recreation photography with a strong emphasis on the West. Her photographs have been published in such magazines as *Outdoor Photographer, Adventure West, Bicycling, Excursions,* and *Peterson's Photographic.* She is an avid camper and hiker and lives in Del Mar, California.

3

CONTENTS

INTRODUCTION

When we mention camping to a friend of ours, he immediately recalls Navy survival training where he was sent into the desert wilderness for three days with one match and a pat on the back. Other people's idea of "roughing it" might be a night at the nearest hotel. There are many

Tent camping

versions of camping, ranging from virtual homes on wheels, to National Parks with all the basic amenities, to bike camping or back country hiking where the only voice you hear is your own. This book does not promote one mode over another, but will show even the most entrenched city dweller how to enjoy life in the outdoors with a minimum of struggle.

We'll help you wade through the maze of equipment on the market today and teach you how to plan your trip, including tips on traveling with children.

Camping with your entire house

Camping brings people together

We'll give you practical, up-to-date information on first aid and advise you on how to safeguard yourself against animals and the elements. A camping trip wouldn't be complete for us without great food, so we've also included a section on easy gourmet fireside menus.

Camping is a sport that can be pursued in varying degrees by people of all ages. It provides relief from the stresses of our high tech world, and it's a great way to teach children about nature. Camping brings families together by providing an inexpensive activity that can create fond memories.

People of all ages enjoy camping

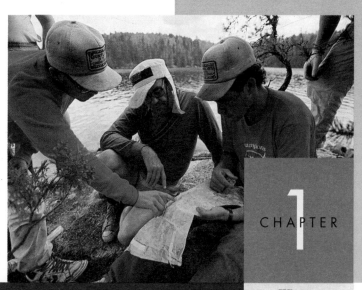

PLANNING YOUR TRIP

Whatever "camping" means to you, your pleasure can be enhanced by some common-sense planning. This means deciding who's going, what type of camping you're going to do, where you're going, and when. Advance reading gives you the benefit of someone else's trial and error, and also creates anticipation and excitement. A little time spent doing research up front can prevent hours of frustration on the road.

CAMPING COMPANIONS

The first question that needs to be asked is "Who are my camping companions going to be?" Choose your camp mates carefully – if people are stubborn, inflexible and finicky at home, they will be even more so on the road. If children or neophyte campers are joining the group, they would probably be better suited to car camping or horsepacking, which allow for more conveniences. Keep in mind driving distances; children tend to get antsy after a few hours in the car. If the purpose of the trip is to find a little solitude, then keep the number down. If your group is too large, it's harder to achieve compatibility, and decision-making time is vastly increased. Talk beforehand to share information and determine everyone's level of experience and fitness.

Camping is a great way to teach children about nature

Disabled Campers

If anyone in your group is disabled, there are some special accessibility considerations. Organizations like the Sierra Club and Access America publish an atlas and guide for visitors with disabilities that includes information on

Disabled campers can be accommodated

trails, parking, and restroom accessibility (see Directory at end of book). Rails to Trails is a special program that is turning old railroad tracks into trails for wheelchair bound campers.

Canine Companions

Canine companions can make great camping buddies, but check regulations for your destination to inquire about leash laws and tick infestation. Make sure Bowser has had all his shots and has current address tags in case he gets lost in the woods. If you're headed to bear or mountain lion country, pets are better left at home for their safety.

Check ahead for pet restrictions

Solo Trips

Solo camping has its advantages, but more planning is in order. The more experience you have camping with others, the better qualified you are to go it alone. Remember, all of your experiences, good and bad, become more intense when you're by yourself.

CAMPING STYLES

The amount of planning needed is determined by the type of camping you're doing. If you're going by car, the "To Do" list is much smaller, and you can take more along, like that bottle of dry white wine to go with the spinach-stuffed trout. Canoe camping and horsepacking also allow you to take quite a bit of gear. Remember, though: camping is getting away from it all. **KEEP IT SIMPLE!**

If a bike trip or backpacking is on the agenda, then weight and space become a big factor. Everything you bring, you

Camping by car allows you to bring more gear from home

Bike trips require special packing

carry. If you insist on taking your camera and that big zoom lens, then you may have to shave some weight elsewhere. Food/meal planning also becomes more precise with backpacking or biking (see Ch. 6). Thankfully, manufacturers have been diligent about inventing lightweight versions of most necessary items, so even if you're on a seven-day trek through the wilderness, you can eat well and be comfortable. It's a good idea to make a trip to the nearest outdoor store for the latest gadgets. You may want to do a short pre-trip trial run locally to get used to riding your bike with loaded panniers or saddle packs. The same goes for the backpack. Try hefting your pack fully loaded to check the distribution of weight and your stamina while carrying it.

Know your limits and plan ahead

13

Pre-trip Equipment Check

No matter what type of camping you choose, check all equipment ahead of time. This means that the car, bike, tent, canoe, etc. are in good working order. Try out new equipment in the backyard to get used to its operation. Being on the trail at dusk, hungry, is not the time to have to pull out the directions and figure out how to start the stove. Arrive at your campsite early enough to set up during daylight hours.

WHERE TO GO

Probably the most exciting part of planning a trip is deciding where to go. The U.S. is so varied, offering everything from RV (recreational vehicle) campgrounds, to National Parks, to primitive sites, that there is truly something for everyone. Ask friends or employees at the local camping store for recommendations. Check newspaper travel sections or magazine articles for ideas. Make sure to take note of the difficulty rating of trails. The National Park Service, and both state and local chambers of commerce, can provide a wealth of information on campground facilities, as well as a calendar of festivals and local events. Always make a trip to the bookstore or library before you break out the gear. Get everyone involved in the planning, including children. Do plan on visiting a map store or your local AAA (American Automobile Association) for a good set of maps. Nothing is more aggravating than wasting time arguing about getting lost (unless you want to get lost). Map Link in Santa Barbara has 90,000+ domestic and international titles, and, if you have

The most exciting part of planning a trip is deciding where to go!

access to a computer, the Internet provides a wealth of information at the touch of a button. America Online has a travel library and GORP – Great Outdoor Recreation Pages – is a good starting point for general information on all outdoor activities. Adventure Sports and Back Country are two other home pages that have comprehensive lists of survival schools, wildflower hotlines, and backpacking trails (see Directory at end of book).

For your initial forays into the sport of camping, pick a destination within a few hours of your home. You might want to travel on more scenic byways on the way there, and use the highways for the way back if time gets short. Make sure to find your location or that "secret spot" on the map before leaving. If you can't find it on the map, you probably won't be able to find it once you're in the woods.

Primitive Campsites

Traveling to primitive campsites requires more thorough planning with regard to extra food, water, and first aid supplies. If you forget something, be prepared to do without, or be inventive. With a little imagination, most items can pull double duty if necessary.

International Camping

If your travel plans include an overseas adventure, check with that country's embassy for necessary visas, and call the Center for Disease Control in Atlanta (tel: 404-639-3311) to find out about suggested inoculations. Don't assume that personal supplies such as contact lens solution, medications, hygiene products, batteries, and toilet paper can be found overseas, especially in third world countries. Most travel guides have sections on campgrounds, and Map Link in Santa Barbara, CA has maps for international destinations.

Rejoice and participate in nature rather than try to conquer it.

SEASONAL CONSIDERATIONS

The time of year you choose also plays a part in preplanning. As this is a beginner's guide to camping, we won't delve into winter camping, but seasonal factors are important. Is it the rainy season? How cold will it be? Are the wildflowers blooming? Are the fish biting? Is it peak tourist season? Does the campground close down after Labor Day? Camping has become such a popular sport that sometimes it's necessary to

Winter camping requires special skills

make reservations at popular National Parks months in advance. If you are locked into peak times because of work or school vacations, plan on arriving at your destination as early as possible to get the best choice of campsites.

Whatever mode of camping you choose, wherever your destination, the amount of time spent doing a little preparation and research before you hit the road has a direct correlation to your "fun quotient." Your pleasure will be enhanced by a willingness to slow down, breathe deep, and enjoy mother nature's many offerings.

BASIC EQUIPMENT

CHAPTER 2

How much gear is necessary for a camping trip? For the beginning camper, the limitless range of equipment available in the stores can be overwhelming. One of the beauties of camping is the chance to take a vacation without spending a lot of money. This chapter will help you wade through the trendy advertisements and hoopla, to choose equipment that will get you started in the sport without taking out a second mortgage on the house.

19

THE BASICS

When shopping for equipment, remember to stick to the basics: tent, sleeping bag and pad, stove, cooking utensils, lantern, first-aid kit, and a few other miscellaneous items. If backpacking is on your agenda, additional items like packs, water filters, and sturdy hiking boots will be on your shopping list. Gear can be expensive, so you need to decide how much to spend on these items. A good rule of thumb is to buy the best quality that you can afford. Another option is borrowing or renting equipment if you're unsure of liking the sport.

Tents

The green canvas pup tent from your scouting days is a thing of the past. The vast array of tents on the market will amaze you, and so will some of the prices. Plan on spending $90 - $350, depending on your particular size needs and tastes. When choosing a tent, keep in mind the type of camping you'll be doing, the number of people who will be using the tent, and the seasonal rating – whether its materials are suited for a range of weather conditions. If you'll be car camping, weight is not an issue. The smaller dome tents are perfect for 1-4 people, and are easy to set up. If your

Dome tents are easy to set up

Grouping a few small tents together gives everyone some privacy

family is large, should you go with one big tent or a couple of small ones? Again, this is entirely up to you. Sometimes having a couple of smaller tents is more fun. It gives everyone some privacy, and it makes the kids feel like they're out on their own, while also teaching them some responsibility in setting up camp. If most of your camping will be done in spring, summer, and fall, you won't need to spend the extra money for a four-season tent. Even if winter camping is not in your plans, a tent will need to withstand wind, rain, hail, and possibly snow, so it should be made of high-quality material and come with a *rain fly* – a separate canopy that is placed over the top of the tent to keep it dry.

When shopping for a tent, go to a camping specialty store and look at the ones set up as floor displays. Crawl inside them, lay in them – is it roomy enough? Is it sturdy? Are the seams sealed? Have the salesperson show you how to

Use your tent's rain fly even if it's not raining – to reduce condensation

set it up and take it down while you're in the store. Most tents
have 2-3 poles held together by elastic cord, which are thread-
ed through sleeves, making camp set-up a cinch. There are
even a few models that practically set themselves up when
shaken out of their bag! It's a good idea to buy a ground tarp
to put underneath the tent to keep the floor from getting wet.
Choose a tarp with metal-ringed holes, or grommets, around
the edges, so rope can be attached to erect a canopy on
rainy days.

Sleeping Bags

A sleeping bag is the next big purchase, and there are
plenty of styles to choose from. The type of camping you'll be
doing will determine the bag style, the temperature range, and
the insulation material. If you're going to be doing any backpacking or bike camping, the more compact, lightweight

mummy bags are a must. Some people, however, find mummy bags too restrictive. Also, it's nice to have the rectangular bags that can be zipped together to form a nice, cozy cocoon for two. All sleeping bags are temperature rated. A good rule of thumb is to buy a bag with a comfort rating of 10 degrees *lower* than the coldest temperature you plan to encounter, which will probably be around the freezing mark. This will keep you warm on those unseasonably chilly mountain nights, and in warmer climes, you can always unzip it, or lie on top.

The next consideration is whether you want down (feathers) or synthetic insulation material. The more expensive down bags offer more warmth with less weight, more compactibility, and greater durability. The down side (no pun intended) is that they're also useless in damp, wet weather due to longer drying time than synthetic bags.

Two sleeping bags zipped together make a cozy cocoon for two

A sleeping bag's outer shell fabric will also be a factor in your buying decision. At the cheaper end of the spectrum, shell fabric is usually nylon or polyester taffeta. Mid-range bags are constructed of a new microfiber material, which is a tightly woven fabric that is water-resistant and breathable. At the top end, bags with DryLoft® shells are more expensive and heavier, but are windproof, and more water-resistant and breathable than other shell materials.

Sleeping Pads

In addition to your sleeping bag, you'll want to invest in a quality sleeping pad that will prevent the "princess and the pea" syndrome. There are foam sleeping pads that will do the job,

Self-inflating sleeping pads

but nothing beats the self-inflating models. These pads come in a variety of thicknesses and lengths, and some even have no-slip surfaces to keep you from sliding off onto the cold ground in the middle of the night. They perform double duty as a camp chair with an accessory that is sold at most camping stores. As long as we're on the subject of sleeping, a small

pillow can add a little luxury to the camping experience. A stuff sack filled with clothes or a down jacket covered with your cotton T-shirt works just as well, too.

24   Foam pad doubles as chair seat

Camping Stoves

After taking care of your basic needs of shelter and warmth, your next thoughts will probably turn to food. A lot of meals can be cooked over an open fire, but it's good to have some sort of stove for quick meals, or when firewood is unavailable. The standard Coleman® stove and its competitors are a camping staple, and range from a single propane burner, to the deluxe three-burner models. They're durable, reliable, and use either propane or liquid fuel. Backpackers tend to favor the white gas stoves because they burn hotter, so less fuel needs to be taken along.

Basic camping equipment should include a standard stove and cooler

Coolers

If you're traveling by car, a cooler will be next on your list of necessary items. If you don't already have one, size and price will be your main considerations. The lids on brand-name coolers seem to be better insulated, resulting in fewer trips to the ice machine. Some have a partial flip-top lid, allowing access to drinks or snacks without opening the entire top. Remember, block ice lasts much longer than cubes!

Cooking Utensils

The amount of cooking gear depends on the size of the group, and the type of camping you choose, but there are basics that should be included in your "kitchen box." There are numerous cook kits on the market that are reminiscent of

A cleverly packed kitchen box can hold most utensils

your early scouting days. These come complete with two pots, a frying pan, and one lid that fit neatly in a zippered pouch for storage. There are more elaborate sets that contain plates, cups, and sometimes a large coffee pot made of blue speckled enamel, that evoke images of Ol' Blue, Shorty, and the rest of the cowhands on the big cattle drive. Some people use paper plates and plastic utensils, but it's better to invest in some sturdy plastic plates, bowls and metal utensils, so as not to add to the trash disposal problem. Other cooking necessities include a can opener, pot holder, dish towels, spatula, wooden spoon, waterproof matches or a lighter, and a Swiss

army knife or other sharp knife. Heavy-duty foil, large plastic trash bags, a sponge, and biodegradable dish soap are also needed. Bring plenty of zip-close bags, as these will undoubtedly become your best camping companion. An extra non-stick frying pan, although not essential, will add versatility, especially with a larger group. Your best bet is to make a camping gear checklist to guarantee that nothing is forgotten (see end of this chapter). When traveling by car, a sturdy, rectangular plastic container with a snap-locking lid is perfect for storing food and cooking gear. It keeps everything organized, and safeguards your food from small animals once at the campsite. These can be found at most discount and hardware stores.

Everything but the kitchen sink? Make a checklist and stick to it!

Lanterns

Camping light sources range from lanterns, to flashlights and headlamps, to candles. If you have the room, it's good to include at least one of each of these as part of your gear. There are various styles of lanterns on the market today. The brightly burning propane lanterns are convenient and quick to light – matches are not even required with the newer ones. These burn on two cloth mantles which, unfortunately, are fragile, and useless when broken, so bring extras. There are also battery-operated lanterns with fluorescent light tubes. They don't put out as much light as the propane lanterns, but they aren't as fragile either, and can usually be recharged by simply plugging into your car's cigarette lighter.

Flashlights are a necessity, and the multi-paks of various sizes are a good value. Having multiple flashlights planted in strategic places assures you of being able to find them when needed. An adaptation of the old miner's headlamp is becoming popular, and it's great when that third hand just isn't available to hold the flashlight. Remember to always take extra batteries. Candles add a little romance to the campsite and are an

Remember to take extra batteries

almost weightless, secondary light source for those who are backpacking. Remember to bring extra matches in a water-proof container.

Head lantern

Propane-burning lantern

Water Filters/Purifiers

If you are backpacking, you will also have to decide on a method of water purification. Those clear mountain streams are not as benign as they seem, and can harbor contaminants

that can wreak havoc on your intestines. Water can be boiled, but that takes time and uses a lot of fuel. Iodine tablets are another method, and their only drawbacks are the delay time and

Water filters guard against harmful impurities

the slightly unpleasant taste. There are various portable filters on the market that take care of giardia and other impurities found in the rivers of the U.S. If you're traveling to other countries, especially third-world destinations, a water purifier is the safest route. In addition to filtering the water, a purifier also uses chemicals to elim- inate any viral contaminants. There are a few different brands and sizes, so check with your local adventure store for all the details.

Boil water to purify it

Miscellaneous Items

There are a few other items that need to be included on any camper's list. These include a good first-aid kit, a day-

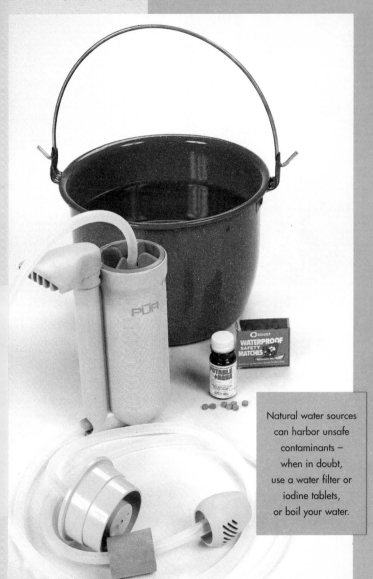

Natural water sources can harbor unsafe contaminants – when in doubt, use a water filter or iodine tablets, or boil your water.

Keep it light and don't overdo it

pack, compass, rope and/or bungee cords, and trail maps. A camp chair of some sort will make lounging by the lake much more comfortable. Bring a tarp to go underneath your tent, and an extra blanket to ensure comfort during unseasonably cold or wet weather. A deck of cards or miniature games for kids will come in handy for the evening's entertainment. And don't forget a favorite book – camping is the perfect time to catch up on your favorite reading.

That's it for bare bones equipment. As you camp more, you'll find all kinds of nifty gadgets that will make you wonder how you ever got along without them. But, camping isn't about taking the whole house, including the electric can opener, with you. It's about enjoying the serenity of nature as a comfortable minimalist.

Ahh... the tranquility of the great outdoors!

MASTER CAMPING LIST

The following is a checklist of possible items – *not* meant to ALL be taken with you. As you camp more, you will develop a more refined list that fits the needs of you and your group.

Main Items

- ❏ books
- ❏ camera
- ❏ candles
- ❏ chairs
- ❏ clothes
- ❏ cooler
- ❏ daypack
- ❏ extra batteries
- ❏ extra blankets
- ❏ extra mantles
- ❏ extra socks
- ❏ flashlights (3)
- ❏ games
- ❏ hatchet
- ❏ hiking boots
- ❏ lantern
- ❏ matches
- ❏ pillows
- ❏ rope
- ❏ sleeping bags
- ❏ sleeping pad
- ❏ stove
- ❏ stove fuel

- ❏ stuff sacks
- ❏ sun shower
- ❏ Swiss Army knife
- ❏ tarp
- ❏ tent
- ❏ tent rain fly
- ❏ tent stakes
- ❏ trail maps
- ❏ water containers
- ❏ whistle
- ❏ _____
- ❏ _____
- ❏ _____
- ❏ _____
- ❏ _____
- ❏ _____
- ❏ _____
- ❏ _____
- ❏ _____
- ❏ _____
- ❏ _____
- ❏ _____
- ❏ _____

Kitchen Box

- ❏ aluminum foil
- ❏ biodegradable soap
- ❏ can opener
- ❏ cooking fuel
- ❏ cook kit with pots & pans
- ❏ cutting knives
- ❏ dishcloth, towels
- ❏ eating utensils
- ❏ hot pads
- ❏ large plastic trash bags
- ❏ measuring cups & spoons
- ❏ paper towels
- ❏ plastic cups
- ❏ plastic plates
- ❏ plastic tablecloth
- ❏ resealable plastic bags
- ❏ scouring pad
- ❏ serving utensils
- ❏ spatula
- ❏ spices
- ❏ wash basin
- ❏ waterproof matches
- ❏ water purifier
- ❏ wooden spoons
- ❏ _____
- ❏ _____
- ❏ _____
- ❏ _____

Bathroom Box

- ❏ adhesive bandages
- ❏ alcohol swabs
- ❏ allergy medicine
- ❏ aspirin
- ❏ biodegradable soap
- ❏ dental floss
- ❏ deodorant
- ❏ fingernail clippers
- ❏ first aid kit (see Ch. 5)
- ❏ gauze
- ❏ hand lotion
- ❏ hygiene products
- ❏ insect repellent
- ❏ laundry bag
- ❏ moist towelettes
- ❏ razor
- ❏ sunblock
- ❏ toilet paper
- ❏ toothpaste
- ❏ towels
- ❏ upset stomach remedies
- ❏ washcloths
- ❏ _____
- ❏ _____
- ❏ _____
- ❏ _____
- ❏ _____

CHAPTER 3

SETTING UP CAMP

Okay, so you've done all the planning, bought the necessary equipment, packed the car, and hit the road. The next step will be to set up camp. Some people spend as much time deciding on a campsite as they do choosing a neighborhood. This seems reasonable, considering that your camper or tent will be your vacation home for your days on the trail.

Finding a campsite and setting up camp are

probably the most important aspects of low-impact land use. If you plan to be in an established campground, the layout of the sites is done for you, and the basic amenities of a picnic table, fire ring, water source and bathroom facilities will be provided. At that point, your only considerations will be which site has the best view, and how close is it to the bathrooms and other campers.

CHOOSING A SITE

If you are backpacking, you'll have a little more latitude in designing your campsite; however, there are some basic rules to follow. Keep in mind that topography does vary with the seasons. Last year's dry wash or quietly babbling brook may be this year's raging torrent, especially after a mountain storm.

If the topographical map indicates a lake, check for feeder streams or springs. Otherwise, during dry times, that little pond may dry up completely, or become a swampy mosquito hatching area. When choosing a spot, it's best to camp in a site that has been used before by other campers, rather than carve out a new one. It'll do less damage to the environment and be less work for you as well.

Select an area that is out of sight of the trail and 200 feet away from any fresh water source. Find a spot that is soft enough to drive in tent stakes, and

Never camp this close to water

Remove any rocks, twigs or pinecones – you'll sleep a lot better

position your tent so that you do as little damage to the vegetation as possible. Grassy sections are more resilient than those with woody undergrowth. Start by removing any rocks, twigs, or pinecones – a small pebble that seems insignificant to the eye can result in a very uncomfortable night. Next, put a tarp down that is slightly smaller than the floor of the tent. This safe-guards the tent from getting wet on damp or rainy days, prevents wear and tear on the tent floor, and extends the life of the waterproof coating. It's nice to position the opening of the tent to greet the morning sun, and you'll also want to take advantage

Grassy ground recovers more quickly from campers

of surrounding views. It's a good idea to use a rain fly even if there's no rain in the forecast. A rain fly will help retain heat,

Room with a view

prevent condensa-tion, and keep your tent dry if a storm comes up quickly. Stake both the tent and the rain fly to avoid seeing your tent roll away like a tumbleweed in a sud-den gust of wind. If

the ground is too hard or rocky for stakes, put a rock in each corner of the tent. The rain fly can be staked by attaching cord to the grommets, pulling it taut, and tying the rope around logs or rocks. Pounding nails into trees for your tarp or laundry is a definite no-no! Do not dig a drainage ditch around the base of your tent, either – it scars the land.

**COOKING
AT PRIMITIVE
SITES**

In addition to the sleeping area, you'll also want to designate a "kitchen." At established campgrounds, there are usually picnic tables and fire rings. Sometimes barbecue grills are provided. Although it is usually quicker to cook meals on a stove, some people feel that cooking over an open fire heightens their outdoor experience. Campfires also make a great gathering place for storytelling and star gazing – not to mention marshmallow roasting!

There are a few things to consider when deciding whether or not to have a fire: the suitability of the site, availability of wood, weather conditions, local regulations, and fire danger. In sites where there are existing fire rings, use them. You can, however, build one

Use existing fire rings when possible

by clearing away a four-foot radius of dry twigs, and placing rocks in a circle. Make sure there are no low hanging branches overhead. When finding wood for the fire, gather it from a wide circumference so that no single area becomes stripped. Use ONLY deadfall, those loose pieces found on the ground.

Most people think of a campfire as a huge, roaring blaze. Actually, the best fire for cooking is one that provides consistent, even heat. This is accomplished by steadily adding small sticks to the fire – none larger than a person's wrist. If the weather is extremely windy or the conditions are dry, a stove should replace the fire as a means of cooking. Check with local authorities about forest fire danger due to drought. One spark on dry pine needles is all it takes to wipe out a forest.

BUILDING A FIRE

To build a fire, first gather a good supply of different sizes of dry wood, and have it ready. This is a great camp chore for kids. The starter is called *tinder*. Tinder is small bits of material that are lighted first to get the flame going. Dead grass, dry pine needles, dead leaves, or paper can be used. Fuzz saved from your dryer screen at home also works well. Build a small tepee around the tinder using very small twigs, or *kindling*. Remember: fires need air to burn. Add slightly larger sticks, keeping the tepee shape. Light the tinder from the upwind side, with the wind blowing away from you towards the fire. When the fire is burning nicely, gradually add larger branches.

Most people can build a fire with dry materials, but what if it's wet? Outdoor stores sell fire starter in a tube, which helps jump start the flame, but it's no substitute for dry kindling. If the fire goes out because of damp wood, don't keep wasting fire starter. Stop, and start over from the beginning, being sure to use dry tinder and kindling. You may have to walk further afield to find dry branches under a tree or rock ledge. Once the fire is burning, you can place larger logs a

tinder

small twigs or kindling

larger branches

couple of feet above the flame, balanced on piles of rocks. This not only forms a canopy to protect the fire from rain, it dries out those larger logs as well. When it's time to put out the fire, thoroughly douse the flame with water, stir the ashes with a stick, then douse again to

Know how to properly extinguish a fire

drench any stubborn sparks. If water is in short supply, use dirt to smother the fire, but take care to stamp it with your boots to truly suffocate and extinguish any remaining embers. **NEVER, EVER LEAVE A FIRE UNATTENDED.**

SAFEGUARDING FOOD FROM ANIMALS

The cooking area should be downwind from your tent to avoid late night encounters with unwelcome critters. Wild animals are not polite enough to wait for an

Enjoy nature without feeding the animals

invitation to dinner, and are very adept at gnawing their way into packs for tidbits. When enjoying nature, a good rule to follow is: **DON'T FEED THE ANIMALS** – no matter how cute they are. Keep your food in air-tight plastic containers or double resealable plastic bags. Dispose of food scraps properly by feeding them to your canine companion, or burning them completely in a hot fire. Or, better yet, eat everything on your plate and become a member of the "clean plate club."

Most campgrounds in bear country have locking metal bear safes to stash your food. If you're backpacking in bear country, check with rangers before hitting the trail to determine if there are *bear-proof wires* at any of the sites. The

Better to lose your food than tangle with a bear

wires are steel cables strung between two trees about 20' high. You will need about 50 feet of rope and two stuff sacks. Divide your food equally between the two stuff sacks. Throw

How to store food provisions using bear-proof wires

one end of the rope over the cable, and tie a stuff sack to the other end. Hoist the stuff sack about 20 feet into the air. Tie the remaining stuff sack to the rope as high as you can. Don't leave any rope hanging; put it inside the sack. Using

Hang your food from a tree...

the pole that is normally provided, push the lower sack up until the two are both about 15 feet off the ground. The sacks will be too high for bears to reach, and the cable is too thick for them to break. In the morning, use the same pole to push one sack up until the other one is low enough to reach. If there are no bear proof wires, use the same concept, but throw the rope over a high tree limb or cliff ledge. If you are unable to safeguard your stuff sacks, remember that it is better to lose your food than tangle with a bear.

...or lower your food over a cliff

KITCHEN CLEAN-UP

When it's time to clean up, never wash dishes in a lake or stream. To keep from polluting the water when washing your dishes, perform this activity at least 200 feet from any water source. Utilize large collapsible water containers to avoid repeated trips to gather water. Put two drops of biodegradable soap in the largest pot, and use it as your sink to wash all utensils and plates. If you've forgotten your sponge, dry pine needles make an excellent natural scouring pad. Continue to use the same washing spot about 20-30 yards away from camp, and when disposing of dirty water, scatter it on the ground at least 200 feet from fresh water. Any garbage that cannot be burned should be packed out and disposed of properly – not left for park rangers or subsequent campers.

Burn or pack out your garbage

45

BATHING

Sometime during a long trip, you may begin to wonder whether there is a correlation between the smell of your dirty, dusty body and your lack of close friends. At this point, your thoughts may turn to bathing. Long ago, in the old West, some tough guys bathed only a few times a year, and they wore the same long underwear until it fell apart. Although this is certainly an option for modern campers, it's not a require-

You don't have to wait for a camping trip to enjoy a portable sun shower

ment. However, sudsing up in a pristine lake or stream is also unacceptable. Even biodegradable soaps can wreak havoc on fragile aquatic ecosystems. Use a portable sun shower – a plastic water pouch with a little nozzle. Fill the pouch with water; lay it in the sun until warm; hang it on a branch, and enjoy! Or, heat up some water on the stove and have a campmate pour it over you as you scrub. When you really yearn to jump in the lake, make sure you rinse off well first. If you simply must wash clothes, and there's no laundromat in sight, wash garments

Nature provides plenty of clothesline

in a pot or ziploc bag filled with heated, soapy water. Scatter the waste water in the dirt, at least 200 feet from fresh water.

WASTE DISPOSAL

Proper disposal of human waste is also crucial to avoid pollution of the environment. Follow the example of cats, and dig a hole 6-8" deep in an inconspicuous place at least 200 feet from camp, trails, and water supply. When finished, cover with dirt and leaves. Use unscented toilet paper sparingly, and then burn it completely in a hot fire or pack it out and dispose of it at the nearest waste station. Never bury it. The same rules apply for feminine hygiene products. If you're part of a group, or staying at the same spot for a few days, dig a trench and follow the same procedure.

BREAKING CAMP

When the time comes to break camp, the main objective is to leave no trace of your stay. Burying, dumping, or leaving trash is not acceptable. Comb the site for bits of paper, and pack everything out, including litter left by others. Any remaining food scraps should also be picked up from the kitchen area and packed out. Make sure that the campfire is completely out, and scatter the cold ash over a wide area. Replace all logs and rocks that were moved when you set up camp. Leave the area as good as you found it, or better.

Take only pictures and leave only footprints

BE PREPARED ON THE TRAIL

During the planning stage of any camping trip, you will gain knowledge about the particular conditions of your destination. Taken a step further, there are important preparedness routines to be aware of, whether you're going for 2 hours or 2 weeks. The more prepared you are – especially for the unexpected – the smoother and more enjoyable your camping trip will be.

TRAILHEAD REGISTRATION

It is estimated that only 1 in 5 hikers registers their party at the trailhead or beginning of the trail. Reasons range from wanting to protect their privacy to hoping to safeguard their parked car against theft or vandalism. However, not only does the register show land management officials which trails are being overused, but it gives rescuers a good lead to your whereabouts if something should happen on the trail. Another basic tool in camping readiness is the detailed itinerary that should be left with a responsible friend or family member. This itinerary should contain a photocopied map of

Register at the trailhead or leave an itinerary

your destination, showing the planned trails and campsites. Indicate where your car will be parked, along with the make and model of the car and the license plate number. Be sure to include the telephone number of the closest ranger station or land management office, and let your contact person know the date of your return. Remember to give him/her a call as soon as you get off the trail.

HIKING ESSENTIALS

There are some essential items that should be taken along on any foray into the woods, whether you're going on a nicely marked National Park trail or a trek through the backcountry: water, food, whistle, map and compass, knife, matches, warm clothes, rain gear or large plastic trash bags and first-aid kit. With these essentials, you can survive a night or two in the wilderness if lost. Also remember individual precautions if you are sun sensitive or allergic to bees, etc. If you're biking or boating, don't forget the all-important repair kit – mechanical things have a tendency to break down and test your trail ingenuity in the best of times.

Hip packs and day packs carry all you will need on the trail

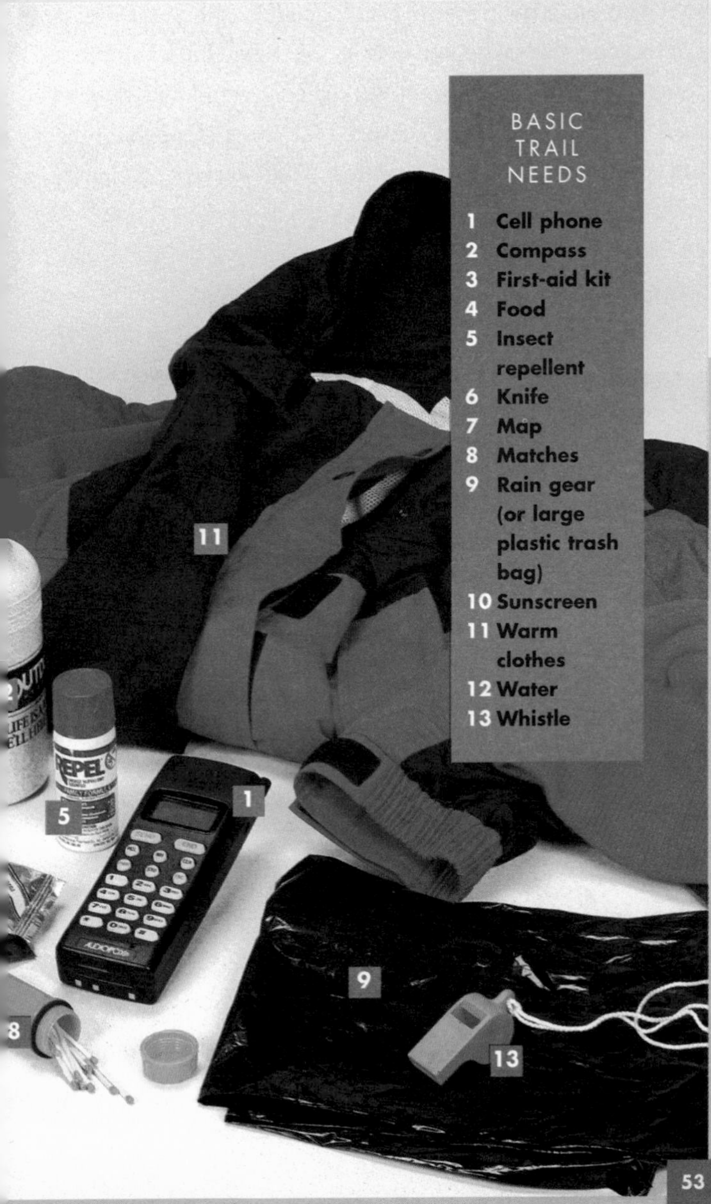

BASIC TRAIL NEEDS

1 Cell phone
2 Compass
3 First-aid kit
4 Food
5 Insect repellent
6 Knife
7 Map
8 Matches
9 Rain gear (or large plastic trash bag)
10 Sunscreen
11 Warm clothes
12 Water
13 Whistle

With the growing popularity of cellular phones, there is controversy over whether they should be included on the "must take" list. An informal survey conducted by *Backpacker* magazine (April '96 issue) showed that the purists barely won out over the cell phone advocates. While most people go camping to get away from technological stress, cellular phones can be valuable when emergencies arise, especially when traveling alone. They allow rescuers to give initial medical advice, and help them determine your location. In addition, a representative at SOLO (Stowe Outdoor Learning Opportunity), a search and rescue school in New Hampshire, says that cell phones give rescuers an opportunity to assess the severity of a situation to determine whether or not to initiate a full-fledged rescue effort, or just to give the hikers enough information to help themselves. Keep in

Cell phones are not a substitute for trail savvy

mind the cell phone's limitations. The batteries may run down, or there may not be a cell in that area. The cellular phone should NOT be viewed as a substitute for backwoods savvy and basic first aid knowledge. Use it as a backup device only.

HIKING WITH A GROUP

Once you're ready to hit the trail, check with rangers first and listen to their advice about weather, fire danger, and trail closures. Some considerations if you're traveling with a group:

1. Discuss fears and phobias beforehand – group support and common sense help everyone enjoy the trip

2. Be flexible – cater to the needs of the group

3. Check your ego at the trailhead – this is not a contest

4. Stay together – the slowest person sets the pace

5. Let everyone take their turn leading on the trail

6. If separated, stop at forks and wait for others

Be flexible, share leadership, and stay together

7. Share leadership and decision-making responsibilities

8. In an emergency, the most experienced hiker takes the lead

55

CLOTHING

There is no such thing as "normal" weather conditions in the mountains. Freak snowstorms or thunderstorms can come up suddenly when skies are robin's egg blue as the hike begins. Even on pleasant days, temperatures can vary greatly between morning and afternoon or with a change in elevation, so layering is the best defense against the elements.

The four layers of clothing consist of:

1. Underwear
2. Clothing
3. Insulation
4. Outer protection

Today's design of thermal underwear has kept pace with technology, and the lightweight synthetic polypropylene is

favored among many outdoor enthusiasts because of its breathability and its ability to wick moisture away from the body. The clothing layer can be anything from wool to one of the new "miracle fibers" on the market such as Cordura, Supplex, or Polartec®. The big advantage of these new synthetic fibers is their quick drying time. Cotton is not recommended as it absorbs water

Dress appropriately

and doesn't dry quickly. For insulation, top off your ensemble with a lightweight parka or fleece vest. In case of bad weather, an additional outer layer of some sort of rain gear is essential – it can be as humble as a trash bag with holes cut for

Layer with a lightweight parka and hat

head and arms, or as expensive as a Gore-Tex® parka. Gore-Tex® earns its reputation as a miracle fabric by letting perspiration

Keep feet dry and protected

escape through tiny pores, but not letting water inside. Always splurge on good, thick socks made of an acrylic/nylon/wool blend, and take along an extra dry pair, too. Wet, sweaty feet can cause unnecessary burning and blisters on the trail.

UNEXPECTED WEATHER CHANGES

If it does rain on your "parade," beware! Even if the temperature is 60 degrees, a body doused by rain can become hypothermic. Don't wait – deal with it promptly! (See Ch. 5 for details on treatment for hypothermia.) Find shelter out of the elements, under a rock overhang or embankment. If there is no shelter around, use extra trash bags as tarps.

Get out of wet clothes fast, and, if possible, start a fire and drink hot liquids to warm your body temperature. Avoid alcohol – it dehydrates as well as dulls the senses. Don't feel pressured to continue if weather conditions are not to your liking. Set up camp, and get your pack out of the rain to keep your spare clothes and your sleeping bag from getting wet.

Be prepared for all types of weather

INSECTS AND ANIMALS

In addition to weather, plants, insects, and animals also command respect, and pre-trip planning should include familiarization with local flora and fauna. Learn to recognize poison ivy and its cousins, and steer clear. Insects, though usually not deadly, are bothersome. Bring along insect repellent, and, if traveling to tick- infested areas, take extra precautions to lessen contact with these

Tuck in your pants to keep insects out

unpleasant little creatures. Wear light-colored, long-sleeved shirts and pants for easier detection. Scoff at the "fashion police" and tuck your pants into your socks, leaving no exposed skin at grass level. Wear insect repellent on your clothing and check each other once or twice daily.

Bug screens are another option

Bears

In bear country, remember that you are an intruder in their habitat. While hiking, make plenty of noise (or wear bells around your wrists or ankles) and keep in mind that there is safety in numbers. Avoid dense cover, and travel in open areas when possible. Never be careless with food when camping in bear habitats. Most National Parks provide locking metal bins for food storage. When in the back country, hang food in stuff sacks suspended from a rope or tree limb (see Ch. 3). Never store food, or cook it, in your tent. Don't sleep in clothing that contains food odors. When you see those adorable little cubs, remember that an angry, protective mother is not far off. Whatever you do, don't surprise them or approach them at their kill or food cache. Some signs of irritation a bear will make, like yawning, head swinging, and looking down, let you know that you're too close. If a bear woofs, the situation is very dangerous. Back away very slowly. Don't run; bears can outrun humans easily. Some people carry bear repellent – a hot pepper spray that should be aimed at a bear's eyes and mouth from a moderate distance. Bear repellent, available in hunting or outdoor stores, has proven to deter serious trouble when properly used.

LOST ON THE TRAIL

Even with good trail planning, it's possible to get lost. Sometimes trails are poorly marked or signposts are destroyed, and some animal trails or drainage ditches look more like trails than the real thing. If the trail seems to peter out, go back to the last visible section, check your map, and try again. If hiking over rocky areas, look for *cairns* (rocks stacked as trail markers). Get advice from hikers coming from the opposite direction as

Cairns are rocks stacked as trail markers

to the time and distance to your destination, as well as the condition of the trail. If backpacking is your game, beware of shortcuts. The terrain can be questionable, and it usually takes longer to reach your destination. Not only does off-trail hiking require more energy, but your chances of getting lost are greater.

Keep in mind that high altitude equals thin air, and, therefore, the need for more rest. If you do get lost, **DO NOT SEPARATE** from your companions or your pack. You may need to spend the night

If you get lost, never separate!

there, and you'll need your gear. Also, unless there are life-threatening circumstances like fire, **STAY PUT!** Try to find a highly visible area like a nearby hilltop or meadow to make it easier for rescuers to find you. Leaving an itinerary with a trusted friend ensures that search teams will be alerted, and will know where to begin looking for you if you don't return on time. Sending out a search aircraft is very expensive and is usually the last resort in a rescue effort. Search and rescue teams tend to look for signs first, and then lost hikers. Depending on the terrain, there are ways to improve your chances of being located by rescuers:

DEEP WOODS

Whistle – According to SOLO, whistles have saved more lives than any other device. Remember the international distress call... three bursts, pause, three bursts.

Fluorescent Surveyor's Tape – This is a lightweight addition to your pack and highly visible even in heavily forested areas when tied around trees near your spot.

Signal Fires – Three fires built 50 feet apart in a triangular formation is an international distress symbol and useful in an air search. Just the smoke from one fire is enough to alert rangers to your location, so carry a firestarter kit and waterproof matches.

MOUNTAINS/SNOW

Whistle – (see above)

Signal Fires – (see above)

Ground-to-Air Distress Symbol – To form this universal symbol, use any available material such as logs, stones, etc., and form three straight vertical lines (I I I) that are big enough to see from the air.

DESERT/SNOW

Ground-to-Air Distress Symbol – (see above)

Signal Mirror – The mirror only works in the desert or other sparsely vegetated areas, and is dependent on sunny conditions. Look through the sighting hole, keeping the airplane or rescuers in the center. Move mirror to reflect the sun and produce three flashes, pause, three flashes.

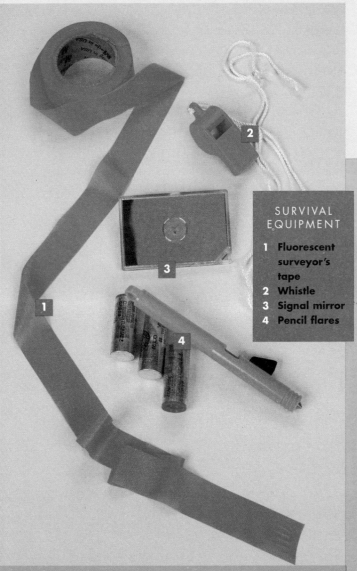

SURVIVAL EQUIPMENT

1 **Fluorescent surveyor's tape**
2 **Whistle**
3 **Signal mirror**
4 **Pencil flares**

Whether you're going for 2 hours or 2 weeks, the more prepared you are for the unexpected, the smoother and more enjoyable your trip will be.

63

Pencil Flares – Flares have limited effectiveness in snow, heavy rain, high winds, and dense forest canopy. They shoot skyward and burn for 8 seconds, so wait until rescue aircraft is in sight.

These preparedness routines and rescue techniques are important to know, but the best insurance against an emergency is prevention. Be familiar with the area, and know your limits. Your gear is only as good as you are – know how to use it! Mother Nature can be brutal at times, and can put your knowledge and fortitude to the test. Be ready.

FIRST AID

On the majority of camping trips, the most serious first-aid treatments will probably be for insect bites, sore joints and muscles, minor burns, heat exhaustion, and possibly, frostbite. This chapter will cover these maladies and other more serious conditions such as shock, hypothermia, severe wounds with external bleeding, as well as the basics of CPR.

FIRST AID KIT CONTENTS

The chances of experiencing a life-threatening injury are small, but emergencies do happen. The key is to be prepared with basic first-aid knowledge. Always carry a first-aid kit while camping

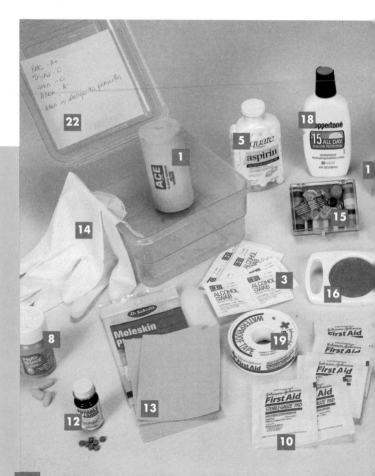

or backpacking. Take a smaller version on day hikes, as well. There are plenty of ready-made first-aid kits on the market, complete with a guide on treating most general illnesses and injuries. If you want to put together your own kit, here are some basic contents you should include:

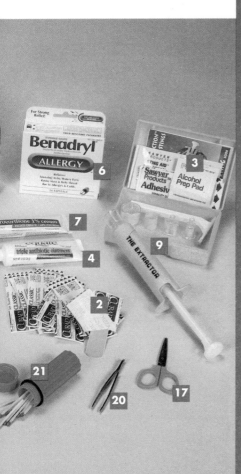

1 Ace® bandages
2 Adhesive bandages
3 Alcohol swabs
4 Antibiotic ointment
5 Aspirin
6 Benadryl®
7 Cortisone ointment
8 Diarrhea medicine
9 Extractor™ (for snake and insect bites)
10 Gauze bandages
11 Insect repellent
12 Iodine tablets
13 Moleskin for blisters
14 Plastic gloves
15 Sewing kit
16 Small mirror
17 Small scissors
18 Sunscreen
19 Tape
20 Tweezers
21 Waterproof matches
22 Include a list of everyone's blood type, allergies, and persons to contact in an emergency. Remember personal medications, such as insulin, etc.

Insects

Insect repellents are a good deterrent to mosquitoes and other pests. Check with rangers to see if you're camping in a tick-infested area, and if so, take some precautions to lessen your chances of getting too acquainted with these pests. Wear light-colored, long-sleeved shirts and long pants for easier detection. Apply insect repellent to your clothes as well as your skin.

Apply insect repellent to your clothes as well as your skin

Although not all ticks carry disease, and not all bites result in an infection, some ticks do spread Lyme disease. If a tick has attached itself to you, use tweezers and extract gently, grasping the tick as close to your skin as possible. Wash the area thoroughly, and apply alcohol or iodine. Watch for signs of a red rash around the bite and feelings of fatigue or flu-like symptoms. Seek medical treatment as soon as possible. Lyme disease is curable with antibiotics.

Snakes

Snakes tend to avoid people as much as people avoid them. Again, check with the local ranger to determine if there are poisonous snakes in the area, and learn to recognize them. Don't reach blindly between rocks or under wood piles. Keep your distance, but if a snake does strike, seek medical treatment immediately. If that is not feasible, outdoor stores recommend The Extractor™ – a syringe-like apparatus you place on the skin, directly over the bite to suction the poison. It works for ticks and bee stings, too.

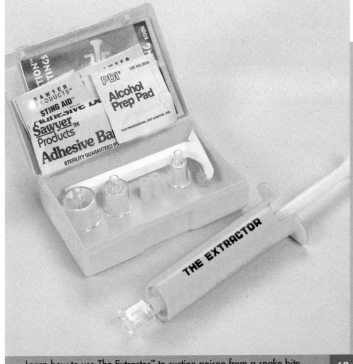

Learn how to use The Extractor™ to suction poison from a snake bite

When faced with a first-aid emergency, STAY CALM. First assess the situation, check for a medical identification bracelet to provide information about the victim's known medical problems, and then determine the most serious situation to attend to first. With many serious injuries or illnesses, there is a high risk of shock. After confirming that the person is breathing, has a pulse, and has no severe bleeding, begin a secondary survey to check for signs of shock.

Symptoms

- **Rapid, weak pulse**
- **Rapid, shallow breathing**
- **Pale, cool, moist skin**
- **Dilated pupils**
- **Dull, vacant stare**
- **Confused behavior**

Treatment

1. Improve circulation by laying the person down.

2. Elevate the feet if no injuries are present.

3. Maintain body temperature by placing a blanket around the body.

Common sense should tell you that with any injury, if symptoms persist or get worse, seek proper medical attention immediately.

BURNS

Getting too close to the camp fire or misuse of lighter fluid or fuel can result in burns. Use caution when starting fires, especially on windy days. The following are symptoms and treatments for various types of burns:

FIRST DEGREE BURNS
Symptoms
- Reddened skin
- Mild swelling
- Pain

Treatment
1. Submerge in cool water or apply cold compresses.
2. Bandage loosely with clean gauze.

If injured, STAY CALM and seek medical attention quickly

SECOND DEGREE BURNS

Symptoms

- **Open or closed blisters**
- **Deep reddening**
- **Swelling/Pain**
- **Wet skin appearance**
- **Signs of shock**

Treatment

1. **Closed blisters:** Flush with cool water until pain subsides. Apply moist bandage loosely.

2. **Open blisters:** Do not use water, as it increases risk of shock and infection. Apply dry, sterile bandage loosely.

3. Keep burned limbs elevated.

4. Provide first aid for shock.

THIRD DEGREE BURNS

Symptoms

- **White or charred skin appearance**
- **Exposed tissue or bone**
- **Signs of shock**

Treatment

1. Leave all clothing and adhered particles on burned skin.

2. Apply dry, sterile bandage loosely.

3. Treat for shock.

When camping in the summer or in desert areas, remember to drink lots of water. We all tend to overdo it sometimes, and our bodies' cooling systems just can't keep up. Follow these treatments for heat exhaustion and heat stroke:

Drink before you become thirsty to stay hydrated, and wear a hat in the sun

HEAT EXHAUSTION

Symptoms

- Pale, cold, <u>clammy</u> skin with heavy perspiration
- Total body weakness
- Headache
- Nausea
- Dizziness
- Possible fainting

Treatment

1. Keep person resting with feet elevated.

2. Loosen clothing.

3. Apply cool, moist towels.

4. Offer sips of cool water if person is conscious and NOT vomiting.

5. Treat for shock.

HEAT STROKE

Symptoms

- **High body temperature**
- **Hot, red, <u>dry</u> skin**
- **Headache**
- **Variable pulse/breathing**
- **Possible convulsions**
- **Unconsciousness**

Treatment

1. Cool person immediately; sponge bare skin with cool water, and apply cold compresses to armpits, wrists, ankles, and neck.

2. Monitor vital signs: pulse, breathing, heart rate.

3. Treat for shock.

When you are enjoying the outdoors, cold weather or freak storms can also pose a threat to your well-being. Be on the lookout for signs of hypothermia and frostbite.

HYPOTHERMIA

Symptoms

- Shivering
- Numbness, weakness, dizziness
- Drowsiness and confusion
- Impaired judgment and vision
- Slow breathing and pulse
- Lowered body temperature
- Unconsciousness

Treatment

1. Shelter person from cold, rain, wind.

2. Remove wet clothing; replace with dry clothing and blankets.

3. Warm the body slowly by huddling closely to the person or by applying warm compresses to the trunk of the body, armpits, and groin.

4. If the person is alert, slowly give liquids (no alcohol).

5. Keep person at rest.

6. Treat for shock.

FROSTBITE

Symptoms

- Skin slightly flushed
- Initial pain which subsides
- Area feels cold and numb
- Confusion or lack of awareness of injury
- Color of affected skin changes to white or grayish yellow, and finally bluish

Treatment

1. Get person to a warm place.

2. Gently immerse frozen area(s) in warm water to rewarm.

3. Do not rub frostbitten area – it may cause extensive tissue damage.

4. After rewarming, gently dry affected area and bandage loosely.

5. Keep person warm without overheating.

6. Monitor vital signs: breathing, pulse, heart rate.

SEVERE EXTERNAL BLEEDING

If, during your primary assessment of an emergency, you discover severe external bleeding, take action to control it.

Symptoms

- Bleeding

Treatment

1. Apply direct pressure to the wound using a sterile bandage or clean cloth.

2. Elevate the injured area above the level of the heart, unless it causes undue discomfort or you suspect a fracture.

3. If bleeding continues, apply pressure point technique:
   Arm wound: while maintaining direct pressure on the wound, locate the pressure point at the brachial artery on the inside of the upper arm. Apply pressure by squeezing the artery against the underlying bone.

   Leg wound: while maintaining direct pressure on the wound, locate the pressure point at the femoral artery in the groin area. Apply pressure by positioning the person on his/her back, if possible, and placing the heel of your hand directly over the pressure point. Apply pressure against the underlying bone.

4. When bleeding is controlled, bandage wound with sterile bandage or clean cloth.

5. **DO NOT** remove bandage – bleeding may restart and/or tissues may be damaged.

When you check a person's vital signs, your primary concerns will be breathing, pulse, and heart rate. The ABC's of emergency care are:

A = Airway – Does the person have an open airway?

B = Breathing – Is the person breathing?

C = Circulation – Is the person's heart beating?

The treatments for obstructed airway, rescue breathing and CPR (cardiopulmonary resuscitation) are:

OBSTRUCTED
AIRWAY

Symptoms

- Person is not breathing
- Chest does not rise and fall

Treatment

1. Open the airway by using the head-tilt, chin-lift method: with one hand on the person's forehead and two fingers under the chin, tilt the head back.

2. While maintaining an open airway, assess breathing by placing your ear over the person's mouth to listen for breaths.

3. Look, listen and feel: look for the chest to rise and fall; listen for breaths; feel for air.

4. Look in the person's mouth, doing a finger sweep, to check for foreign objects blocking airway. If there is a blockage, preform the Heimlich Maneuver (see next page).

5. If person doesn't start breathing, but has a pulse, perform rescue breathing for respiratory arrest (see next page).

HEIMLICH MANEUVER

Symptoms

- **Person is choking**
- **Foreign matter blocking airway**

Treatment

1. Stand behind victim and wrap your arms around his or her waist.

2. Press one fist (with thumb inward) against the abdomen and below the rib cage.

3. Grasp your fist with the other hand and use a quick upward thrust into the victim's abdomen.

4. Repeat until object is dislodged.

RESCUE BREATHING

Symptoms

- **Person is not breathing**

Treatment

1. Maintain open airway.

2. **Adult:** give one slow breath every 5 seconds.
   Child: give one slow breath every 3 seconds.

3. Watch for chest to rise and fall.

4. Continue giving breaths for about one minute.

5. Recheck pulse. If pulse is still present, but there is no breathing, continue rescue breathing.

6. Recheck pulse every minute.

CARDIAC ARREST

If person's pulse stops, provide first aid for cardiac arrest.

Treatment

Location of Compression Position

1. Kneel by the person's chest.

2. With the middle and index fingers, locate the lower edge of the rib cage on the side closest to you.

3. Slide your fingers up the edge of the rib cage to the notch where the ribs come together.

4. Go up 2 fingers higher, and place the heel of your other hand on the breast bone.

5. Place the heel of your other hand directly on top of the first, keeping your fingers off the chest. For a child, use only one hand for compressions.

Compressions for an Adult (ages 8 and up)

For all compressions, if there are two rescuers, give 5 compressions to 1 breath. If there is only one rescuer, give 15 compressions to 2 breaths.

1. Position shoulders over hands, with elbows locked.

2. Compress breastbone 1½ to 2 inches, at a rate of 80-100 compressions per minute, keeping hand contact with the chest at all times.

3. Count aloud with each compression, "One and two and three and four and five...breathe."

4. After a minute, give 1 slow breath lasting 1-2 seconds, and watch for the chest to rise and fall. Recheck breathing and pulse.

5. Repeat compressions/breaths: 10 cycles of 5:1 (if one rescuer, 10 cycles of 15:2).

Recheck pulse, and if no pulse, continue until person's heart begins beating, another trained individual takes over, or you're too exhausted to continue. If person regains pulse but is still not breathing, perform rescue breathing.

Compressions for a Child (ages 1 to 8)

For all compressions, if there are two rescuers, give 5 compressions to 1 breath. If there is only one rescuer, give 15 compressions to 2 breaths.

1. Position shoulder over hand, with elbows locked.

2. Compress breastbone 1 to 1½ inches, at a rate of 100 compressions per minute, keeping hand contact with the chest at all times.

3. Count aloud as compressions are given. For children, the count for compressions is faster, "One, two, three, four, five… breathe."

4. After a minute, give 1 slow breath lasting 1½ - 2 seconds, and watch for the chest to rise and fall. Recheck breathing and pulse.

5. Repeat compressions/breaths: 20 cycles of 5:1 (if one rescuer, 10 cycles of 15:2).

Recheck pulse, and if no pulse, continue until person's heart begins beating, another trained individual takes over, or you're too exhausted to continue. If person regains pulse but is still not breathing, perform rescue breathing.

A good solid knowledge of first aid is important, especially if you are venturing into the backcountry. When hiking, keep your eyes on the trail and keep your hands free to avoid falls. Know your limits, use common sense, and be prepared for a change in the weather. Always carry a first-aid kit with you, and know how to use it.

CHAPTER 6

COOKING

One of the best things about camping is the delicious aroma of a great meal cooking over an open fire, especially if it's the trout you snagged earlier that afternoon in a cold, clear mountain stream. Even if you aren't lucky enough to catch any fish, it is possible to cater to gourmet appetites without lugging along a six-burner stove. Allow for whim and some spices, and you won't have to leave your taste buds at home.

DETERMINING FOOD NEEDS

Camp cooking can be accomplished with little effort and expense, and like everything else, the more you do before you go, the less of a struggle it will be on the trail. This chapter will show you how to prepare simple, tasty entrees that will satisfy even finicky appetites. When calculating your food needs, some things to consider before you hit the supermarket aisles are:

- How many people are in the group?
- What is the length of the trip?
- Are you car camping or backpacking?
- Is fishing allowed?
- How many meals will be eaten on the trail vs. at the campsite?
- Does anyone in the group have special dietary needs?
- Are dogs and kids part of the group? (Remember, teenagers eat a LOT!)

Plan a daily menu before you make your shopping list, and be sure to include snack and trail foods in addition to regular meals. Menus are not set in stone; you may want oatmeal for dinner one night instead of stir fry, or you may get lucky at that trout stream after all. To cut down on bulk, after shopping, repackage items in zip-seal bags and label with ingredients, directions, and cooking times. If you group together all the components for each meal and premeasure the ingredients, all that's left to do at the campsite is "just add water" – the experienced camper's cooking mantra. Don't forget about spices and instant sauces – a little curry powder

Planning each day's menu will prevent you from overpacking

Camping food can be simple, inexpensive, and found at almost any food store

or onion soup mix can really jazz up a meal without taking up much space in your pack. The same goes for Parmesan cheese and bouillon. Powdered sports drinks and powdered milk are also easy to pack. Don't forget the staples: flour, sugar and margarine.

READY-MADE CONVENIENCE FOODS

In the past, campers and hikers had to rely on expensive, bland, freeze-dried foods that didn't rate high on the taste scale. Today, not only have freeze-dried foods improved, but there are plenty of quick foods like soups, chili, rice dishes, and oriental special-

Repackage food items in zip-seal bags to cut down on bulk

ties on supermarket shelves. In addition, there are vacuum-packed items, such as ravioli, that are lightweight and don't require refrigeration. Some meals made ahead of time at home, like chili, soups, and stews, can be frozen in plastic containers and then pull double-duty as ice blocks in the cooler.

Follow your ancestors' lead and take advantage of the growing season, utilizing fresh vegetables and fruits, or double the batch when cooking meals at home and freeze or dehydrate half for future trips. If children are part of the group, don't worry about their appetites – they usually are less finicky on the trail and eat more than at home. Encourage a sense of participation by having them help with the preparation and cooking of simpler foods like doughboys or meatloaf on a stick. (See Recipes at end of chapter.)

DEHYDRATORS

If you have access to a dehydrator, you can make dried fruit or jerky for trail snacks. Home drying expands your menu choices considerably, while giving you complete control over preservatives and added sugar. If you don't have a commercial dehydrator, your oven will suffice. Set the oven at 140° or the lowest setting, and prop the door open slightly. Just about anything can be dehydrated, including soups, stews, vegetable puree, and even rice pudding. Just spread the food thinly on a greased cookie sheet or shallow pan and dry for 6-8 hours or overnight. Once at the campsite, "just add water!" Dehydrated foods are great for backpackers where weight is a concern, and lightweight, filling meals are needed.

Dehydrators expand menu options

MAXIMUM ENERGY FOOD GUIDELINES

While camping, and especially backpacking, a little more attention should be paid to caloric intake to provide maximum energy on the trail. Depending on body size, you should aim for a 4000+ calorie-a-day diet consisting of a majority of carbohydrates for quick energy.

Try to avoid empty calories. For optimal performance, your diet should consist of 70% carbohydrates, 15% protein, and 15% fat. Calories from carbohydrates (sugars and starches) break down quickly into glucose for fast energy. Unfortunately, the body's storage capacity for carbs is small, so it needs a regular intake. You shouldn't go more than a couple of hours without a snack, so keep them handy. Fig bars, dried fruit, gorp or trail mix, and energy bars are all good choices. A high-carbohydrate diet a few days before leaving on your trip helps augment glycogen stores. Foods rich in carbohydrates include whole grain breads, cereals, applesauce, pasta, beans, peas, fruits, oatmeal, vegetables, brown rice, juices, lentils and potatoes.

Carbohydrates provide lasting energy

Some protein in your diet is also important because it contains amino acids necessary for tissue maintenance.

Protein takes more energy to digest, and also releases energy over a longer period of time. Unused protein (which is usually not a problem on hiking or camping trips) becomes fat. Some foods containing protein include fish, chicken, eggs, yogurt, beans, legumes, cheese, nuts, soy products, hummus, peanut butter, salami, and meat jerky.

Chicken and fish are a good source of protein

A little bit of fat is needed for cooking, as well as in your diet. Fat makes you feel full and satisfied on the trail, and any calories will be burned off while hiking. Butter is the least practical choice as it becomes rancid in hot weather unless it's clarified first. Margarine is much better because it stores well even in hot temperatures and can be purchased in convenient, leak-proof squeeze bottles. Olive oil is another good choice. It, too, stays fresh in hot weather; just be sure to repackage it in a leakproof bottle and place in a zip-seal bag for extra insurance against spills. Imitation butter flakes are another, but less popular option. They are good to add to foods while dehydrating, but are not good for frying.

COLD FOOD STORAGE

Once on the road, be aware of food storage guidelines. When you're car camping and have a cooler, your only concern is to keep an eye on the ice supply. Block ice lasts much longer than cubes, and, as mentioned before, you can use plastic containers filled with frozen stew or soup as cooling blocks at the beginning of the trip. While backpacking, you obviously won't be carrying food that needs to be refrigerated unless it's packed in an insulated container and eaten the first night on the trail. Do keep your pack in the shade to protect other perishable items. Tents heat up like a greenhouse, so it's best to find a shaded area under a large tree or rock overhang. If there's a mountain stream nearby, place items in tight, waterproof containers and submerge until ready to use. This works great as a wine chiller, too.

Frozen soups and stews can act as ice blocks at the beginning of a trip

NATURE'S BOUNTY

While camping, be open to some of nature's edible gifts. Wild blueberries, strawberries, and raspberries are a delight. Fresh mint is abundant in damp wooded areas, and sage and rosemary lend fragrance and pizzazz to grilled meats and other dishes. Dandelion leaves make for a great salad and are easily recognizable. Wild onions are also readily available in certain parts of the country. But unless you are an experienced botanist, restrict your foraging to these known, common items. Edible wild mushrooms are not worth the risk – there have been too many fatal ingestions.

Cooling bottles in a stream is a natural way to refrigerate

Fresh-picked, wild blueberries – one of nature's many bountiful gifts

BREAKFAST RECIPES

Now, without further ado, let's get to the recipes. Recipes that can be prepared beforehand are marked with a .

Don't be afraid to improvise or add spices according to your family's tastes.

Pancakes

There are plenty of ready-made mixes in the supermarket. If you'd like to make pancakes from scratch, this is a pretty basic recipe.

4 heaping spoons flour	**1 spoon dry milk powder**
½ cup water	**1 egg, beaten**
2 spoons oil/margarine	**• dash of salt**

Mix the flour, milk powder, and salt. Add the beaten egg and oil to the dry ingredients and stir. Batter will be lumpy. Gradually stir in ½ cup water. The batter will be thick. Add more water, if necessary. Cook on hot griddle.

Serves 2-3 people.

Wake up to homemade pancakes hot off the griddle!

Additions: Chop apples, raisins, or other dried fruit into the batter; or add chocolate chips, cinnamon, bananas, wild blueberries, etc.

Granola

3 cups rolled oats	¼ cup melted butter
1 cup shredded coconut	1½ teaspoon cinnamon
1 cup chopped nuts	½ teaspoon salt
¼ cup honey	1 cup raisins

Combine all ingredients except raisins in a mixing bowl. Spread on a greased cookie sheet and bake at 325° for 25-30 minutes, or until lightly browned. Cool and add raisins. Eat with yogurt or milk. Granola also makes a good snack .
Makes 6 cups (1½ pounds).

Camper's Oatmeal

You can use instant oatmeal or the five minute brand. Follow directions on the package. Add nuts and presoaked dried fruit to oatmeal as it is cooking. Serve with brown sugar or honey and warmed milk.

Breakfast Sandwich

½ English muffin	• egg salad
1 slice boiled ham or Canadian bacon	1 slice cheese (Swiss, American or cheddar)

Toast English muffin in frying pan. Spoon prepared egg salad on toasted side, then layer with ham and cheese. Cover and heat until cheese melts.
Makes 1 sandwich.

Morning Mix Up

- **2 cups frozen hash browns**
- **½ cup diced onions**
- **1 cup shredded cheddar cheese**
- **salt & pepper**
- **1 cup diced ham**
- **2 tablespoons oil**
- **6 eggs**

Sauté hash browns, onions and ham in oil until tender. In a separate bowl, mix eggs and seasonings; then add to potato mixture. Cook until eggs are set. Stir in cheese before serving. *Serves 2 people.*

Fresh donuts are a snap!

Sugar Donuts

- **1 package Hungry Jack® biscuits**
- **vegetable oil**
- **sugar & cinnamon**

Heat oil in fry pan (enough oil to cover ½ of donut). Open biscuits, poke a hole through the center of each, and form into a donut shape. Cook donuts in oil until golden brown; flip and brown other side. Dip in sugar or cinnamon/sugar mixture.

SNACK
RECIPES

GORP (Good Old Raisins 'n' Peanuts)

This is a traditional trail snack and is as individual as you are. Some ingredients may include (but are not limited to):

- raisins
- coconut
- M&M's® chocolate candies (plain or peanut)
- mixed nuts
- toasted oat cereal
- dried fruit (banana chips, apples, apricots, prunes)

Mix together equal part ingredients and store in a sturdy, zip-seal plastic bag. Keep it handy for great on-the-trail snacking!

GORP – a traditional trail snack that's fun to make and great to eat!

Campfire S'Mores

A classic campfire favorite!

- **graham crackers**
- **marshmallows**
- **chocolate bars (or chocolate frosting)**

Place a piece of chocolate bar and 1 roasted marshmallow between two graham cracker halves. Gently squeeze together, bite, and have s'more!

Banana Boat

- 1 **banana**
- **small marshmallows**
- **chocolate chips**

Cast your vote for a banana boat!

Slice banana – in the peel – lengthwise, down the center, but not completely through. Spread banana open and alternate marshmallows and chocolate chips until banana boat is full. Wrap in aluminum foil and heat, upright, in campfire. Banana boat is done when chips and marshmallows are melted. Garnish with whipped cream, berries or nuts. Eat with a spoon right from the banana boat peel!

What's camping without the classic S'Mores!

Camping cuisine can be as original and inventive as you make it

Fruit Pockets

- 1 **package crescent rolls**
- 1 **can fruit pie filling (apple, peach, blueberry, etc.)**
- • **2-inch wooden dowel (or clean stick)**

Carefully wrap one crescent roll around end of dowel, making sure to seal close the tip. Cook slowly over campfire until golden brown. Carefully slip roll off dowel and spoon the (warmed) pie filling into the cavity.

Variation: chocolate and marshmallows make a great S'More Pudge Pie (see p. 104).

Turkey (Beef) Jerky

It's easy to make jerky at home, something our ancestors have known all along. Jerky is prized for its travelability.

3 **pounds turkey breast**	½ **cup soy sauce**
½ **cup Worcestershire sauce**	¼ **teaspoon salt**
1 **teaspoon onion powder**	1 **clove garlic, minced**
• **ground pepper**	

Slice the meat thinly, across the grain. Mix remaining ingredients into a marinade and marinate meat for up to 12 hours. Place meat in a dehydrator or warm oven (140°) until completely dried (meat should snap in two when you bend it). Eat jerky plain as a snack, or add it to stir fry or stews. Jerky is a good protein source when you're hiking.

ENTRÉE RECIPES

Herb-Stuffed Trout

There are as many variations of this favorite dish as there are fishermen. Use your imagination and enjoy!

- 1 trout, cleaned and deboned
- • rosemary or tarragon
- • lemon slices, if available
- 1 clove garlic, chopped fine
- 1 teaspoon margarine or oil
- • salt & pepper to taste

Rub the fish cavity with oil, and stuff with herbs and garlic. Wrap the fish in heavy-duty foil and place on the grill or directly on the coals. Cook for 7 minutes on one side, then flip, and cook for about 4 more minutes.

Variations:

Watercress-Stuffed Trout

Stuff the cavity with fresh watercress, finely chopped nuts, thinly sliced wild onions, and a little oil. Place lemon slices on outside of fish and add 2 tablespoons

One fish... two fish... let's eat!

of white wine before wrapping in foil.

Oriental Trout – Baste trout cavity with mixture of soy sauce, garlic, ginger, and sesame oil. Wrap in foil and cook.

Meatloaf on a Stick

This recipe is a hit with kids; they can each cook their own
meal over a campfire.

- **2 pounds ground beef or turkey**
- **2 eggs, beaten**
- **½ teaspoon Worcestershire sauce**
- **2 slices bread, broken into small pieces (or 1 cup bread crumbs)**
- **1 large onion, chopped**
- **½ teaspoon garlic powder**
- **• salt & pepper to taste**

In large bowl, mix all ingredients. Find sticks about 1" in
diameter (wash sticks before cooking). Pat the meatloaf mixture around the stick in a cylinder shape about 1½ inches
thick all around. Wrap the meat in double thickness of aluminum foil and hold over coals turning regularly. Check for
doneness after 10-15 minutes.

Kids will love making their own meatloaf on a stick and weenie wraps

Weenie Wraps

1 package hot dogs

1 package crescent rolls

Skewer a hot dog onto a stick and roast over campfire until warm. Wrap one crescent roll around warm hot dog and pinch edges closed. Continue cooking over the campfire until crescent roll is golden brown. Dip in ketchup, mustard and relish.

Trail Stew

A delicious, hearty meal perfect for campfire gatherings. Cook in large pot using a tripod over the fire, or stovetop. This dish can also be made ahead and frozen to be used as an ice block in the cooler.

Cooking outdoors can be an adventure

Or, just brown the meat beforehand to avoid the messy grease clean up at your campsite.

1 pound ground beef or turkey	**1 small onion, chopped**
1 clove garlic, chopped	**1 envelope onion soup mix**
1 can green beans	**1 can corn**
2-3 potatoes, diced	**4-5 carrots, diced**
1-2 cups water	

Brown ground meat, onions, and garlic. Add remaining ingredients and simmer until vegetables are done.

Pizza Pudge Pies

Pudge pies are fun to make and easy to prepare. Any pizza topping you like can be added to this recipe for a one-of-a-kind treat! A Pudge Pie iron can be found at most camping equipment stores.

- 1 **pound Italian sausage, cooked**
- 1 **(15 oz.) jar pizza sauce**
- • **black olives**
- 1 **pound shredded mozzarella cheese**
- 1 **package sliced pepperoni**
- • **mushrooms**
- • **margarine**
- • **bread slices (try wheat and rye, as well as white)**

Butter two slices of bread. Place one slice, buttered side down, in the iron. Spoon pizza sauce in the center of the bread and top with your favorite pizza toppings – sausage, mushrooms, olives, cheese, etc. Be careful not to fill the pie too full! Place the other bread slice on top, buttered side up, and squeeze iron closed. Cook over the campfire a few minutes on each side, checking often. Pudge Pie is done when bread is golden brown.

Pudge Pie Filling Variations:

Reuben – corned beef, thousand island dressing, Swiss cheese, and sauerkraut

Cheesy Dog – American or mild cheddar cheese and bite-size hot dog pieces

Taco – taco-seasoned ground beef, refried beans, cheddar cheese, tomatoes, black olives, and salsa

Pudge Pie irons make one-of-a-kind meals and treats. Be inventive and encourage kids to help with fillings.

Shishkabobs

Shishkabobs are a fun way to get everyone involved in the meal. Kids enjoy skewering their own creation and watching it cook on the grill. Be creative with different meats and vegetables.

- **4 chicken breasts (cut in chunks and marinated)**
- **2 cans whole potatoes**
- **2 green peppers, chunked**
- **20 large fresh mushrooms**
- **12 cherry tomatoes**
- **8 corn-on-the-cob chunks**

Alternate meat and vegetables on 4 metal skewers and place on grill. Turn frequently and baste with marinade until meat is cooked through and vegetables are crisp-tender. Reserve some marinade for dipping.

Marinades: Italian dressing, soy sauce, teriyaki sauce, lemon and garlic butter, or seasoned olive oil all work well. The only rule to a marinade is never to dip from the same bowl of marinade you've used for basting. Experiment and enjoy!

Nature provides a breathtaking view for even the simplest meals

**BREADS AND
SIDE DISHES**

Doughboys

This old scouting recipe is great for breakfast or dinner.

- **2 cups biscuit mix**
- **½ cup water**
- **• butter or margarine**
- **• jam, honey, grated cheese**

Add water to biscuit mix. Pat a handful of dough around the end of a stick (stick should be at least 2 feet long and ½ inch in diameter; wash sticks before cooking). Toast over coals, turning constantly for about 10 minutes, until inside is done. Gently pull doughboy off the stick, and fill cavity with butter, jam, or other meltable goodies.

Dumplings

Dumplings add substance to any soup or stew and require no extra pans.

- **1 cup biscuit mix**
- **¼ cup water**

Mix the dough and drop by spoonsful into simmering soup or stew. Cover and let steam for 15-20 minutes until the middle of the dumpling is dry.

Cashew Rice Curry

A simple, filling meal for those long days on the trail.

¼ cup powdered milk	½ teaspoon salt
1 ½ teaspoons curry powder	2 ½ cups water
1 cup rice	¼ cup cashew pieces
2 oz. cheddar cheese	

Mix powdered milk, salt, curry powder, and water. Bring to a boil. Add rice and cook over medium heat for 20 minutes. Stir in cashews and cheddar cheese. Serve hot or cold.

NEVER cook inside your tent – it's a fire hazard. Use the vestibule as shown here.

Potatoes in Foil

6 large potatoes, sliced thin	1 large onion, quartered
1 stick butter or margarine	• Lawry's® seasoning

Place potatoes in middle of large piece of heavy-duty foil. Sprinkle with seasoning, dot with butter or margarine, and spread onions on top. Roll ends of foil tightly so steam and juice do not escape. Cook over hot coals about 15 minutes on each side. (Cooking time depends on heat/temperature of fire.) Great with sour cream.

Honey Grilled Vegetables

12 small red potatoes	2 zucchinis, sliced
1 medium eggplant, sliced	1 green pepper, sliced
1 red pepper, sliced	1 large onion, sliced
¼ cup honey	3 tablespoons dry white wine
1 clove garlic	½ teaspoon salt
½ teaspoon pepper	1 teaspoon thyme

Mix together honey, wine and seasonings. Place vegetables in middle of large piece of foil. Pour honey mixture over vegetables. Roll ends of foil tightly, so steam and juices do not escape. Grill 20-25 minutes until vegetables are tender.

Dining on a camping trip can be a delightful experience, and most home recipes can be adapted for the campsite or trail. If your imagination fails you, there are plenty of camping cookbooks on the market.

Oh what a beautiful morning!

CAMP COOKING TIPS

- Pre-measure a recipe's dry ingredients (flour, seasonings, nuts, etc.) into resealable plastic bags labeled with the meal's name. Planning this way is less complicated than loading up on staples, and it reduces waste at your campsite.

- To transport eggs, it's easier to crack eggs carefully into a plastic pitcher or jar with tight lid. When it's time to use the eggs, just pour them out, one-at-a-time, into the pan.

- When group camping, a terrific last night meal is known as the **Chili Dump**. Each family brings enough chili to feed their immediate group members, plus one extra ingredient for the *whole* group to share (shredded cheese, onions, oyster crackers, sour cream, sourdough bread, tossed salad, etc.). "Dump" all chili into a large stock pot or kettle (it may take two pots!) and cook over a low fire for at least one hour, to blend all the different flavors. (The more varieties of chili, the better!) Made beforehand, chili freezes well and acts as an ice block in the cooler.

CAMPING ETIQUETTE

CHAPTER

7

As the wilderness grows smaller, solitude becomes our scarcest resource, and we suffer by becoming jaded and unimpressed by nature. There is always more to learn about ourselves and the wilderness. Learning camping etiquette depends more on attitude and awareness than on rules and regulations, and it preserves our natural resources for future use.

RESPECT THE ENVIRONMENT

When planning your trip, there are steps you can take to minimize your impact on the land. Try to go midweek or off-season, if possible, when crowds are minimal and use levels are low. Remember that the environment is more fragile during snow melt when muddy trails are more quickly eroded. While hiking, walk single file and stay on established trails to avoid damaging new growth. Resist the temptation to cut corners on switchback or tightly turning, steep

Respect the rules – and the environment

trails. It's hard on your knees and erodes the trail. Your route should be carefully chosen to avoid fragile areas and critical wildlife habitats during breeding or hatching times. Traveling quietly in small groups will lessen the disturbance to other hikers and will probably allow you to see more wildlife.

RESPECT WILDLIFE

Speaking of wildlife, all of us have watched cute little chipmunks perform playful antics, and have tossed them a tidbit or two.

Please, **DON'T FEED THE ANIMALS!** This is for your benefit as well as theirs. When fed by humans, animals become habituated, dependent on handouts, and less able to survive on their own. Respect the wildlife, and be aware of how your presence

affects their well-being. Even the harmless approach by humans can be stressful to animals and cause them to use energy that may be needed to forage for food or escape predators. Multiple or prolonged disturbances may cause animals to avoid good feeding grounds or nesting sites. Keep your distance, and enjoy them with binoculars.

SOLITUDE AND PRIVACY

While in camp, respect others' needs for solitude and privacy. Walking through someone else's campsite is like barging through a stranger's bedroom. Go around. If nature's music of rustling trees, chirping birds, and rushing water isn't enough for you, and you absolutely must bring music along, make sure you also bring your headphones. Not everyone shares your taste in music. The fireside sing-along is a charming tradition, but keep it muted, and observe quiet hours if in a campground.

CAMPFIRE PROTOCOL

Another camping tradition is the roaring campfire, but its past misuse and long-term scarring effects are changing the attitudes of many outdoorspeople. Check first with land management officials about the advisability of a campfire. If the conditions are dry and windy, forego the fire and either use a stove, or have a cold meal. If there are no existing fire rings, the best alternative is a mound fire. Locate mound material – sand, gravel, or dirt that contains no vegetation. Using a tarp, gather enough material to create a circular, flat-topped mound 6-8"

Campfires are a fun place to gather... be responsible

thick. Building the fire on this mound keeps the ground from being scorched and the vegetation from being sterilized. When finding wood for the fire, use only downed wood. Small fires create less ecological impact, so save the big bonfires for football pep rallies. Keeping the log size small will assure that no half-burned logs remain as evidence of your presence. All wood should be burned down to ash or very small coals that can be easily scattered when breaking camp.

BREAKING CAMP

When breaking camp, leave no evidence of your site. Pack every thing out, even found litter. Make sure the fire is completely out and the coals are cold, and scatter the ashes over a very wide area. Do not damage any plant life. If you find any natural objects, enjoy them, but leave them where they lie so that others can experience the same sense of discovery. Remember that removing cultural artifacts is illegal. Note their location, and report them to the park rangers upon leaving the park. Leave the campsite as pristine as you found it, so that future campers can experience the full impact of the area's beauty.

VOLUNTEER WORK

In return for the peace and joy the wilderness provides, you may want to put some energy into preservation after you return home. Volunteer with one of the many conservation groups, such as the Sierra Club or the National Park Service, and help with trail maintenance or fund-raising. Or, become involved in the legislative process to preserve our parks. Rejoice and participate in nature rather than try to conquer it. Nature rejuvenates us all, and we need to respect and protect it. Remember to "take only pictures, and leave only footprints."

Volunteers maintain trails and shelters

DIRECTORY AND INFORMATION

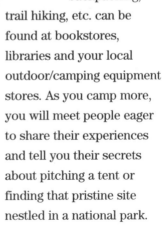

A wealth of information on camping, backpacking, trail hiking, etc. can be found at bookstores, libraries and your local outdoor/camping equipment stores. As you camp more, you will meet people eager to share their experiences and tell you their secrets about pitching a tent or finding that pristine site nestled in a national park.

NATIONAL PARK SERVICE OFFICES

The following park services can help you locate campgrounds and hiking trails in specific areas of the U.S.

Office of the Director
U.S. Dept. of the Interior
NPS
PO Box 37127
Washington, DC 20013-7127
(202) 208-4621

REGIONAL OFFICES

Alaska NPS
2525 Gambel St., #107
Anchorage, AK 99503
(907) 257-2690

Mid-Atlantic NPS
143 S. 3rd St.
Philadelphia, PA 19106
(215) 597-7013

Midwest NPS
1709 Jackson St.
Omaha, NE 68102
(402) 221-3431

North Atlantic NPS
15 State St.
Boston, MA 02109
(617) 223-5001

National Capital NPS
1100 Ohio Dr. SW
Washington, DC 20241
(202) 619-7000

Pacific Northwest NPS
83 S. King St., #212
Seattle, WA 98104
(206) 442-5565

Rocky Mountain NPS
12795 W. Alameda Pkwy.
Denver, CO 80225
(303) 969-2500

Southeast NPS
75 Spring St.
Atlanta, GA 30303
(404) 331-5185

Southwest NPS
PO Box 728
Santa Fe, NM 87504
(505) 998-6004

Western NPS
600 Harrison St., #600
San Francisco, CA 94107
(415) 744-3876

GOVERNMENT AGENCIES

Bureau of Land Management
Dept. of the Interior
18th and C St., #5660
Washington, DC 20240
(202) 208-5717

MAP SOURCES

USDA Forest Service Office
(National Forest Maps)
Public Affairs Office
517 Gold Ave., SW
Albuquerque, NM 87102

United States Geological Survey

(Topographic Maps)
Distribution Section
Denver Federal Center
Building 41
Denver, CO 80225

Trails Unlimited

PO Box 3610
Evergreen, CO 80439
(800) 962-1643

Maplink

12 W. Anapamu St.
Santa Barbara, CA 93101
(805) 963-4438

INTERNET HOME PAGES

Backcountry

(Comprehensive list of information on backpacking and links to other home pages)
http://io.datasys.swri.edu/overview.html

Digital Backcountry

(Information on ordering USGS topographic and other trail maps)
http://www.dnet.net/mbu

GORP – Great Outdoor Recreation Pages

(Starting place for general information on outdoor activities)
http://www.gorp.com

Adventure Sports

(A good general starting point)
http://www.adventure-sports.com

MAGAZINES AND OTHER PUBLICATIONS

National Parks Magazine

(The magazine of the National Parks and Conservation Association)
1776 Massachusetts Ave. N.W.
Washington, DC 20078-6406

Outside Magazine

(Full-color magazine highlighting outdoor recreation)
PO Box 51733
Boulder, CO 80323-1733

GLOSSARY

Cairn – A mound of stones marking trail in treeless area or on a slickrock trail

Deadfall – Dead tree branches found lying on the ground that are good for kindling

Erosion – Wearing away of soil by wind, water, and foot traffic

The Extractor™ – Syringe-like device used to extract poison from insect or snake bites

Feeder stream – Small streams that branch out from main water source

Fall line – The natural downhill course between two points on a slope

Giardiasis – Infection of the lower intestines caused by a bacteria present in "wild" water. The bacteria comes from animal and human waste. Symptoms: stomach cramps, diarrhea, bloating, loss of appetite, and vomiting.

GORP – "Good ol' raisins and peanuts" – high-protein energy snack consisting of nuts, raisins, M&M's® chocolate candies, shredded coconut, and granola or a variation of these

Grommets – Little metal ringed holes in tent or tarp

Kindling – Small twigs used to start campfires

Low impact – Treading lightly on the earth, keeping evidence of your campsite to a minimum

Mantle – Chemically treated mesh sack that fits over propane jet inside a propane lantern and glows when lit

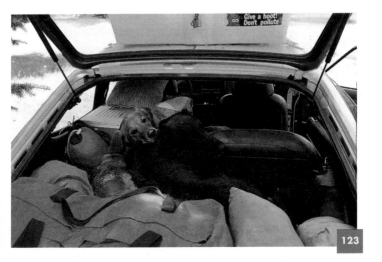

Moleskin – A soft fabric bandage that adheres to feet to prevent blisters

Rain fly – Separate canopy-like piece that fits on the top of a tent to keep rain off

Seasonal rating – Each sleeping bag is rated as to the temperature level for sleeping comfort; i.e., if you plan to camp in winter, you will want a bag with a sub-zero rating.

Switchback trail – A zig-zag trail leading across the fall line on a very steep hill, thereby reducing erosion.

Tarp – Plastic ground cloth placed under the tent to prevent wear and tear on the tent floor and to keep moisture away

Tinder – Firestarter: dead grass, pine needles, dead leaves, paper, etc.

Topo or Topographic map – Shows the elevation of the landscape. From the Greek word "topos" meaning "a place" and "graphien" meaning "to draw."

Trailhead – The start of a trail, usually at a road

Use this Camper's Log to record all your camping adventures!

DATE   **PLACE**

NOTES

DATE   **PLACE**

NOTES

DATE   **PLACE**

NOTES

DATE   **PLACE**

NOTES

DATE   **PLACE**

NOTES

Mount Laurel Library
100 Walt Whitman Avenue
Mt. Laurel, N.J. 08054-9539
(609) 234-7319

PHOTOGRAPH CREDITS

David Rosenberg/Tony Stone Images
Cover

Robert Bossi:
Pages 29, 29 inset a, 60, 83a, 118, 120

Sark Buchaklian:
Pages 23, 27, 28, 31, 41 inset a,b,c, 51, 53, 63, 66, 68, 69, 86b, 87, 89, 91, 92, 96, 97a, 98, 99 inset, 102, 105, 107

Peter Cole:
Pages 16, 18, 19, 26, 28t, 28b, 30, 45, 57a, 58a, 85, 119, 121, 123

Johnson Worldwide Associates:
Pages 4, 11b, 13a, 13b, 18, 20, 21, 65c, 116, 117a, 122a, 128

Layne Kennedy:
Pages 2, 9a, 19a, 19b, 22, 30a, 32a, 32b, 37, 43a, 44a, 44b, 46, 55, 57b, 65a, 65b, 83b, 86a, 88, 93, 97b, 101a, 101b, 106, 108, 111a, 124, 126

The Picture Cube:
Pages 6b, 9b, 16a, 16b, 16c, 16d, 16e, 16g, 16h, 41, 56, 71, 73, 98, 110

Cheyenne Rouse:
Pages 3a, 3b, 15, 16f, 24a, 24b, 25, 26b, 29 inset b, 35a, 35c, 38a, 38b, 47, 48, 49a, 49b, 49c, 50, 54, 61, 83c, 90, 103, 111b, 112, 117b, 112b, 125a, 125 b, 128 inset

Tyler Stableford:
Page 59

Third Coast Stock Source:
Pages 1, 6a, 7, 8a, 8b, 10, 11a, 12,17, 26a, 30b, 35b, 36, 39, 42, 109, 113, 115